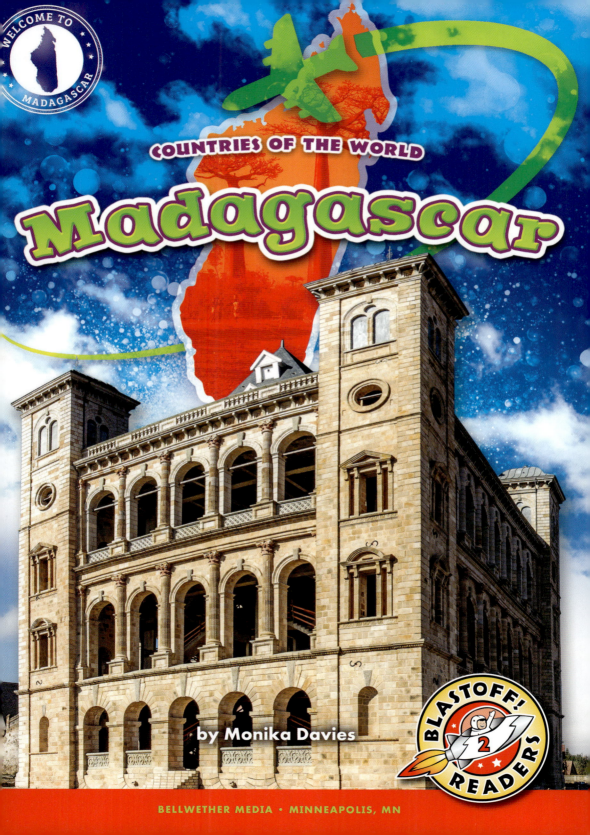

Blastoff! Readers are carefully developed by literacy experts to build reading stamina and move students toward fluency by combining standards-based content with developmentally appropriate text.

Level 1 provides the most support through repetition of high-frequency words, light text, predictable sentence patterns, and strong visual support.

Level 2 offers early readers a bit more challenge through varied sentences, increased text load, and text-supportive special features.

Level 3 advances early-fluent readers toward fluency through increased text load, less reliance on photos, advancing concepts, longer sentences, and more complex special features.

★ Blastoff! Universe

Reading Level

Grade K

Grades 1–3

Grade 4

This edition first published in 2025 by Bellwether Media, Inc.

No part of this publication may be reproduced in whole or in part without written permission of the publisher. For information regarding permission, write to Bellwether Media, Inc., Attention: Permissions Department, 6012 Blue Circle Drive, Minnetonka, MN 55343.

Library of Congress Cataloging-in-Publication Data

Names: Davies, Monika, author.
Title: Madagascar / by Monika Davies.
Other titles: Blastoff! readers. 2, Countries of the world.
Description: Minneapolis, MN : Bellwether Media, Inc., 2025. | Series: Blastoff! readers: Countries of the world | Includes bibliographical references and index. | Audience: Ages 5-8 | Audience: Grades 2-3 |
Summary: "Relevant images match informative text in this introduction to Madagascar. Intended for students in kindergarten through third grade"– Provided by publisher.
Identifiers: LCCN 2024039306 (print) | LCCN 2024039307 (ebook) | ISBN 9798893042290 (library binding) | ISBN 9798893043266 (ebook)
Subjects: LCSH: Madagascar–Juvenile literature.
Classification: LCC DT469.M26 D18 2025 (print) | LCC DT469.M26 (ebook) | DDC 969.1–dc23/eng/20240826
LC record available at https://lccn.loc.gov/2024039306
LC ebook record available at https://lccn.loc.gov/2024039307

Text copyright © 2025 by Bellwether Media, Inc. BLASTOFF! READERS and associated logos are trademarks and/or registered trademarks of Bellwether Media, Inc.

Editor: Suzane Nguyen   Designer: Laura Sowers

Printed in the United States of America, North Mankato, MN.

Table of Contents

All About Madagascar	4
Land and Animals	6
Life in Madagascar	12
Madagascar Facts	20
Glossary	22
To Learn More	23
Index	24

All About Madagascar

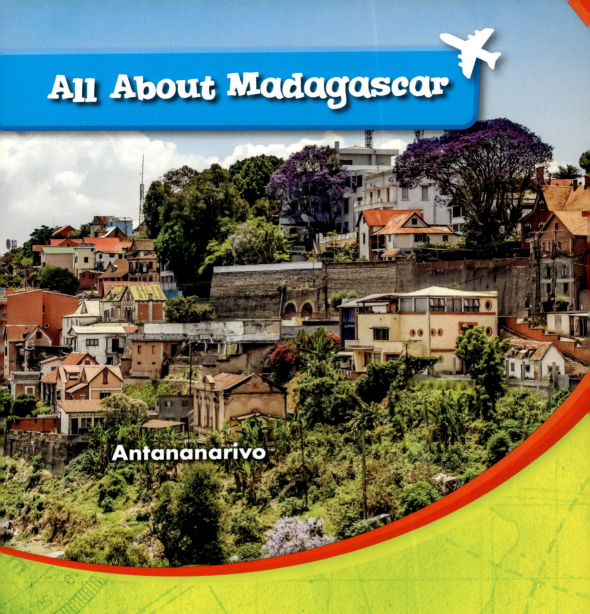

Antananarivo

Madagascar lies southeast of Africa in the Indian Ocean. Its capital is Antananarivo.

It is the fourth-largest island in the world! Many **unique** animals are found only on this island!

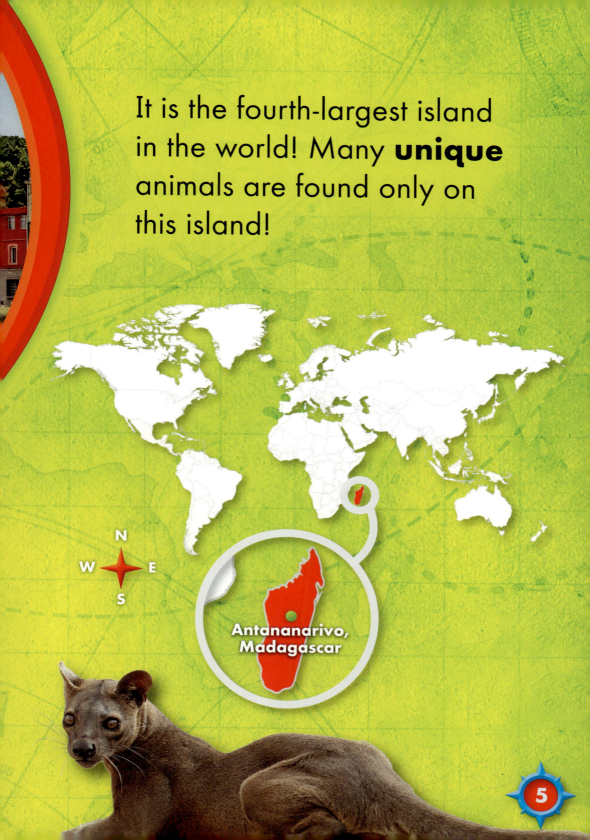

Antananarivo, Madagascar

Land and Animals

A **plateau** covers central Madagascar. A thin **plain** lines the eastern coast. Low and hilly plains stretch down the west.

Mountains stand tall in the north.

plains

Maromokotro

Height: 9,436 feet (2,876 meters) tall
Famous For: the tallest point in Madagascar

Madagascar has two seasons. The dry season is cooler. The wet season is hot.

The central plateau is cool.
Heavy rain falls in the east.
The south is dry.

Thousands of animals call the island home. Partridges look for berries. Red ruffed lemurs hide in trees.

Madagascan sunset moth

Animals of Madagascar

Madagascar partridge

red ruffed lemur

Madagascan sunset moth

fossa

Madagascan sunset moths flutter among flowers. Fossas hunt at night.

Life in Madagascar

Most people in Madagascar are Malagasy. They speak Malagasy and French. **Christianity** is mainly practiced.

Many young people call the country home. Over half of its people are under 25!

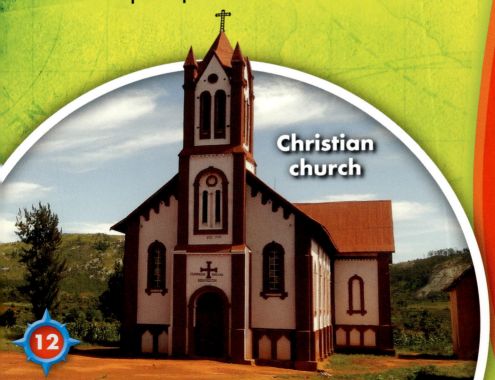

Christian church

Music is important to Malagasy **culture**. The *valiha* is a **traditional** string **instrument** made from bamboo.

People enjoy playing soccer. They also like to go out and meet people.

soccer

Most Malagasy meals are paired with rice. *Romazava* is a meat stew with leafy greens.

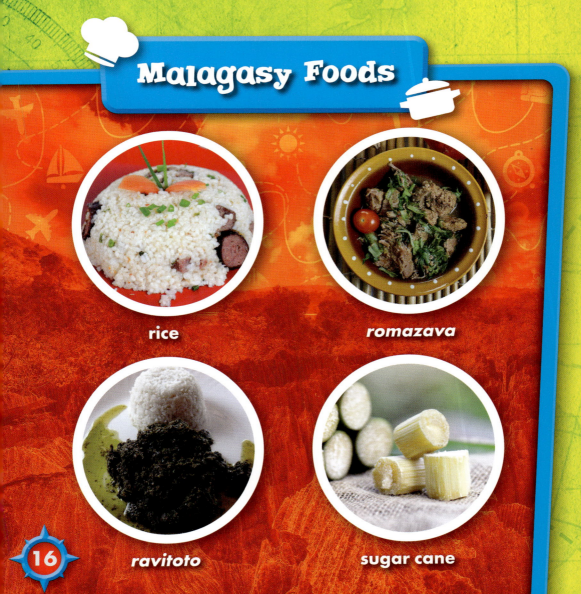

Malagasy Foods

rice

romazava

ravitoto

sugar cane

Ravitoto is ground **cassava** leaves with pork. Sugar cane is a sweet treat!

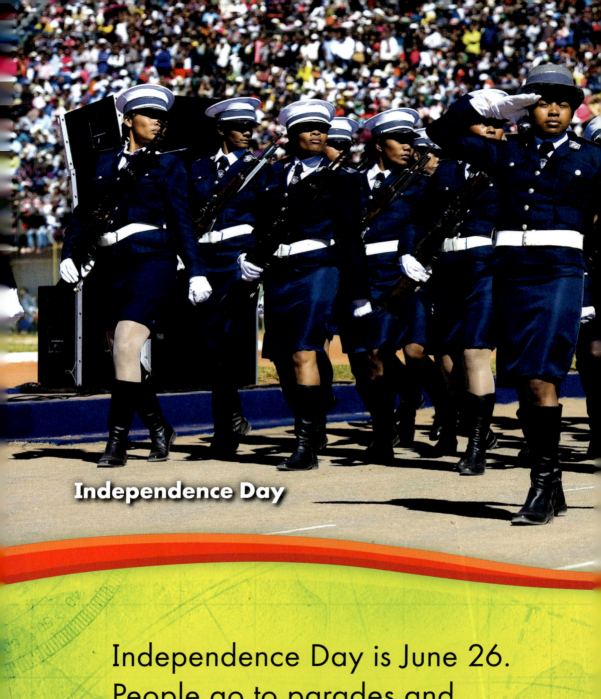

Independence Day

Independence Day is June 26. People go to parades and watch fireworks.

Many people **celebrate** Christmas. They eat, sing, and give gifts. It is a day full of joy!

Madagascar Facts

Size:
226,658 square miles
(587,041 square kilometers)

Population:
29,452,714 (2024)

National Holiday:
Independence Day (June 26)

Main Languages:
Malagasy, French

Capital City:
Antananarivo

Famous Face

Name: Erick Manana

Famous For: singer and guitarist

Religions

- other: 2%
- Muslim: 2%
- none: 22%
- Christian: 74%

Top Landmarks

Avenue of the Baobabs

Royal Hill of Ambohimanga

Tsingy de Bemaraha National Park

Glossary

cassava—a tropical plant with starchy, edible roots

celebrate—to do something special or fun for an event, occasion, or holiday

Christianity—a religion based on the teachings of Jesus Christ and the Christian Bible

culture—the beliefs, arts, and ways of life in a place or society

instrument—a device that makes music

plain—an area of flat land with few trees

plateau—an area of raised, flat land

traditional—related to customs, ideas, or beliefs handed down from one generation to the next

unique—one of a kind

To Learn More

AT THE LIBRARY

Adamson, Thomas K. *Soccer*. Minneapolis, Minn.: Bellwether Media, 2020.

Sabelko, Rebecca. *Butterfly*. Minneapolis, Minn.: Bellwether Media, 2021.

Spanier, Kristine. *Madagascar*. Minneapolis, Minn.: Jump!, 2022.

ON THE WEB

Factsurfer.com gives you a safe, fun way to find more information.

1. Go to www.factsurfer.com.

2. Enter "Madagascar" into the search box and click.

3. Select your book cover to see a list of related content.

Index

Africa, 4
animals, 5, 10, 11
Antananarivo, 4, 5
capital (see Antananarivo)
Christianity, 12
Christmas, 19
coast, 6
culture, 14
dry season, 8
food, 16, 17
French, 12
Independence Day, 18
Indian Ocean, 4
island, 5, 10
Madagascar facts, 20–21
Malagasy, 12
map, 5
Maromokotro, 7
mountains, 6
music, 14

people, 12, 15, 18, 19
plain, 6
plateau, 6, 9
rain, 9
say hello, 13
soccer, 15
wet season, 8

The images in this book are reproduced through the courtesy of: milosk50, front cover, p. 21 (Royal Hill of Ambohimanga); Millenius, p. 3; Elen Marlen, pp. 4-5; Martin Mecnarowski, p. 5; Lubo Ivanko, p. 6; Yann Mayette/ Wikipedia, pp. 6-7; Radodo, pp. 8-9; Luca Nichetti, p. 9; Mark Brandon, pp. 10-11, 11 (Madagascan sunset moth); edevansuk, p. 11 (Madagascar partridge); Artush, pp. 11 (Red ruffed lemur), 15; Martin Pelanek, p. 11 (fossa); szezse1124, p. 12; sunsinger, pp. 12-13; Hello World Stock Library/ Alamy, pp.14-15; gaelgogo, p. 16 (rice); Fanfo, p. 16 (*romazava*); marimos, p. 16 (*ravitoto*); C. Aphirak, p. 16 (sugar cane); GTW, p. 17; Xinhua/ Alamy, pp. 18-19; Foxytail, p. 20 (flag); Domoina RATSARA/ Wikipedia, p. 20 (Erick Manana); KENTA SUDO, p. 21 (Avenue of the Baobabs); Framalicious, p. 21 (Tsingy de Bemaraha National Park); Eric Isselee, p. 22.